SECRET CODES AND CIPHERS

SECRET CODES
AND
CIPHERS

By Bernice Kohn
Illustrated by Frank Aloise

Prentice-Hall, Inc., Englewood Cliffs, New Jersey

Second printing......June. 1969

Library of Congress Catalog Card Number: 68-20368

Printed in the United States of America • J

Prentice-Hall International, Inc., London
Prentice-Hall of Australia, Pty. Ltd., Sydney
Prentice-Hall of Canada, Ltd., Toronto
Prentice-Hall of India Private Ltd., New Delhi
Prentice-Hall of Japan, Inc., Tokyo

For David

CONTENTS

1 Is It a Code or a Cipher?

OD UOY WONK TAHW SIHT SYAS?

If that sentence doesn't make any sense to you, read each word backwards. And if that was too easy for you, try this one:

DBO ZPV SFBE UIJT?

Of course you can. Just change each letter to the one that comes before it in the alphabet.

Both of the "secret" sentences above are in cipher. You don't have to look up anything in a book to find out what they mean. You just have to know the system.

A cipher is always based on a system. The system is a matter of changing the order of letters or words, or of substituting letters or words according to a plan. The substituted letters or words may be *other* letters or words or they may be numbers or symbols. The Morse code, which is used for sending telegrams, is really a cipher, not a code. It substitutes an alphabet of dots and dashes for the letters of the ordinary alphabet.

INTERNATIONAL MORSE CODE

A	·—
B	—···
C	—·—·
D	—··
E	·
F	··—·
G	——·
H	····
I	··
J	·———
K	—·—
L	·—··
M	——
N	—·
O	———
P	·——·
Q	——·—
R	·—·
S	···
T	—
U	··—
V	···—
W	·——
X	—··—
Y	—·——
Z	——··

Samuel F. B. Morse

A code uses substitutions, too, but in a different way. A code uses signs, sounds, numbers, letters or words to stand for words, sentences or complete thoughts. Only rarely does a code use substitutions for single letters. In cipher, X stands for some other letter. In code, X may be a whole word, a whole sentence or the whole message.

A code is never based on a plan that enables you to work it out each time you want to use it. If a code is very simple, you memorize it. You memorize the zip-code number that stands for the name of your area and post office. You memorize your telephone area-code number.

A secret knock on the clubhouse door is code. So are semaphore, or flag, signals (although they may be used as a cipher, too), Indian smoke signals and African drum-beats. They are all memorized by the people who use them.

But most codes are so lengthy and complicated that no one memorizes them. They can be used only with the help of a *code book*. A code book is like a foreign language dictionary. First it has an alphabetical list of all the words or sentences that can be expressed in the code, with the code word or symbol for each one. Then it has an alphabetical list of the code words or symbols and their meanings. Both the sender and the receiver of code messages have to have copies of the book.

While many codes and ciphers in use today are of modern invention, there is nothing new about secret writing. One of the oldest stories about a hidden message goes all the way back to the fifth century B.C. A Greek man named Aristagoras was told that a slave had come to see him. When he entered the house the slave said to Aristagoras, "Shave my head and look thereon." Aristagoras must have been surprised, but he lathered up the slave's head and shaved it clean. There he found a message tatooed on the slave's scalp. It was from Aristagoras's father-in-law in Persia and it told him that the time had come to revolt. Aristagoras did, and the course of history was changed.

A cipher used by Julius Caesar in ancient Rome is still in use today and is still known as the Julius Caesar cipher. It isn't very hard to "crack." In fact, it is very much like the cipher in the sentence

DBO ZPV SFBE UIJT?

But instead of using the letter next to the real one, Caesar moved ahead *three* letters in the alphabet. The same sentence in Julius Caesar cipher reads:

FDQ BRX UHDG WKLV?

In this cipher, when you come to the end of the alphabet you start over at the beginning. That is why the second word begins with B. It is three letters after Y.

Both codes and ciphers can be very simple or very complicated. They can be used for fun or for serious purposes, even for matters of life or death. In the next chapters you will learn about codes and ciphers that you can use yourself, some that are used for business of one sort or another, and some that have dramatically saved or lost lives.

II Secret Codes and Ciphers

Have you ever visited a shop where the price tags read BOK or HLD? This kind of marking is very common in antique shops. The tags don't seem to mean anything at all. Yet, if you ask the price of the rocking chair or the dollhouse, the shopkeeper usually looks at the tag before he tells you.

The secret is code—shopkeeper's code, or cipher. Most stores have set prices for everything and the prices are clearly marked. But in an antique shop, this is often not true. The owner wants to sell for whatever he can get— but he has to be sure that he doesn't lose money. Since it is very likely that no two items in the shop are the same, and there may be hundreds or thousands of them, it is important for the owner to know how much he paid for each article. He writes it down in code or cipher. A glance at the tag gives him his buying price before he tells you his selling price.

Shopkeepers can use any system they like for their codes because, except for a clerk or two, no one else has to understand it. The mysterious letters stand for anything the shopkeeper decides on. But commonly, storekeepers use a cipher. It is based on a ten-letter word that doesn't repeat any letters. Of course, each shop has its own secret word, but the system always works in the same way. Let's say the secret word is BLOCKHEADS. The word is set down and the letters are numbered from 1 to 0.

BLOCKHEADS
1234567890

If the rocking chair cost the dealer $23.00 the tag says LO. If the dollhouse cost $2.50 the tag says LKS. Most ciphers of this sort do not bother with decimal points. The general value of the object makes it clear whether the numbers mean dollars or cents.

One code that you *might* say is used for business is the very old code used by tramps and hoboes as they go from house to house asking for food or money. Since tramps often come to a new neighborhood without knowing how they will be received, they help each other to know what to expect by making small marks near the door with chalk or crayon. Tramp signs are code and they look like this:

8

TRAMP SIGNS

Go

Safe camp

Gentleman

Doctor

Kind woman

Bad dog

Very good

Officer

Guarded house

Stop

Danger

Man with gun

Be quiet

Don't give up

Tell a pitiful story

Judge

One of the most useful codes in business is the commercial code that is used to send overseas telegrams. The charge for such messages is made by the letter so it is important to make the message as short as possible. A commercial code book has lists of short words (five letters is standard) that stand for long sentences. The code word BHRLT might stand for:

YOUR ORDER HAS BEEN RECEIVED. MERCHANDISE WILL BE SHIPPED AS SOON AS IT IS AVAILABLE.

If you look at some business letterheads you will probably see a *cable address* in addition to the regular address. This is usually one word that stands for the name of the company and its complete address, including the name of the country.

But codes are not always used for peaceful purposes. Once, during World War I, an alert radio operator noticed that some of the messages he was sending seemed rather odd. He suspected that they were in code and were being sent by spies. He decided to do something about it.

The next day, the operator was given the message

FATHER IS DEAD

but instead of sending it as written, he changed one word. The wire went out saying

FATHER IS DECEASED

Within a few hours a reply came back. It said:

IS FATHER DEAD OR DECEASED?

There was no longer any question about the messages being code!

Sometimes, even during a war, a code message may show great wit and imagination. Such was the case many years ago when General Sir Charles Napier captured the Indian province of Sindh. It was important that he inform the British War Office, and important that the message not be understood in India. Sir Charles sent a one-word message. It said:

PECCAVI

Fortunately, the man who received the message in England had been an excellent Latin student. He had no trouble at all translating PECCAVI—I HAVE SINNED (I have Sindh). Of course, there must have been many people in India who knew Latin. It was just lucky for the British that the telegraph operator wasn't one of them.

When is it better to use a code and when a cipher? They both have advantages and disadvantages. It is usually faster and easier to put a message into code (*encode*) and to discover the meaning of a code message (*decode*). But code requires a code book, and if it is captured or found, the code isn't secret any more.

Navies use code. The code books are bound in lead, and if the ship is damaged or captured by the enemy, the books are thrown overboard to sink to the bottom of the sea. Sometimes divers have been able to recover the books and learn the code. For this reason, naval codes are changed very often, sometimes every day.

Armies use cipher. It would be dangerous and clumsy for an army on the move to carry around code books. The risk of capture would be very high.

Diplomats, spies, and criminals use both code and cipher, but they use cipher most of the time. With cipher, you can say anything that you can say in your own language. With code, you are limited to what is in the code book.

An easy code to use with a friend is a dictionary code. You must each have a copy of the same edition of the same dictionary. To encode a message, you use numbers instead of words. The number 16:7 means page 16, seventh word.

This is a good "fun" code, but it is only that. During World War I when German spies used a dictionary code, it took American agents only a few days to try out all the German dictionaries until they found the right one and cracked the code.

III Concealment Ciphers

A concealment cipher is one in which the message is concealed, or hidden, in some way. The message that was tatooed on the slave's head was a concealment cipher. It was hidden by the slave's hair.

Messages written in invisible ink are concealment ciphers, too. You can do this kind of secret writing very easily. Write the message in lemon juice and let it dry. The paper will look completely blank until it is held over a hot light bulb. Heat makes the secret writing appear.

There was a time in England when postage rates were very high except for newspapers. People who had little money but plenty of time saved postage by sending letters to their friends with newspapers. They made tiny pinpricks under letters until they had spelled out the whole message.

Soldiers have often used this kind of concealment cipher, too, to tell their families where they were when they weren't supposed to. A soldier would send home a map with a pinprick through the proper spot. The receiver had only to hold up the map to the light to see where the hole was. The system wasn't very successful because the censors caught on quickly. They permitted the maps to go through but they peppered them with hundreds of pinpricks first.

A much better concealment cipher is the *grill cipher* or *Cardan cipher*. It was invented by an Italian mathematician, Girolamo Cardan (or Cardano), in the sixteenth century.

Girolamo Cardan

There are two ways to make a grill. Since both the sender and the receiver of the message need the same grill, you must have a pair of them. The first method is to hold two sheets of paper or cardboard together and cut some holes in them like this:

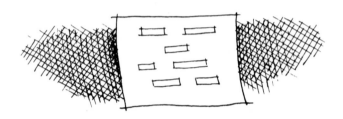

The second way requires graph paper. Number the squares and cut out certain numbers. This is a good method because if you lose the grill, you can easily make another one. To make sure that you remember which numbers to cut out, use your telephone number, an important date in history, or a combination of such numbers. And of course you must always use graph paper with the same size squares.

When the grill is made, place it over a sheet of plain paper and write your message in the holes. Then remove the grill and fill in all the empty space with a make-believe, innocent-sounding message that hides your real message.

Here is an example of a grill cipher. It appears to be a simple letter from one boy to another.

Dear Jerry,

Sorry I haven't written in so long but I'll try to bring you up to date on all the news.

Our baseball team won its first game of the season yesterday. There were three bases stolen. A famous actress came to watch the game and she was wearing beautiful jewels.

My puppies are growing fast and keep me busy. One of them buried a bone and ruined my father's best rose bush. To say that he was angry is an understatement!

Try to come for a weekend visit soon. I'll ask my mother to make your favorite breakfast, pancakes with maple syrup.

> *Your friend,*
> *Steve*

Now let's put a grill over that letter and see what we find.

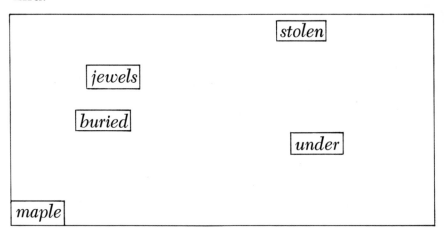

If you found a message that said

LINDA EDWARDS AND VERA EGGERS
TOOK OUR WHITE NOTEBOOKS

you might suspect a concealment cipher. Try to read every other word, the last letter of every word, every fifth letter, etc. When you read the first letter of every word, the message is plain. It says

LEAVE TOWN

As you can see, this is not a very safe kind of cipher to use, but you might have fun with it when absolute secrecy is not important.

Concealment ciphers *have* been used successfully in some very important matters. Long ago, in England during the time of Cromwell, Sir John Trevanion was locked up in Colchester Castle. He had been accused of a crime against his government and was waiting to be put to death. One day, he received the following letter:

Worthie Sir John :- Hope, that is the beste comfort of the afflicted, cannot much, I feare me, help you now. That I would saye to you, is this only: if ever I may be able to requite that I do owe you, stand not

upon asking me. 'Tis not much I can do: but what I can do, bee you verie sure, I wille. I knowe that, if deathe comes, if ordinary men fear it, it frights not you, accounting it for a high honour, to have such a rewarde of your loyalty. Pray yet that you may be spare this soe bitter, cup. I fear not that you will grudge any sufferings; onlie if bie submission you can turn them away, 'tis the part of a wise man. Tell me, as if you can, to do for you any thinge that you wolde have done. The general goes back on Wednesday. Restinge your servant to command.

R.T.

After he read the letter, Sir John asked if he might go to the chapel to pray, since his last hour was at hand.

His jailers granted the request and waited for Sir John to finish his prayers. When several hours passed, they entered the chapel to find it empty.

After studying the letter carefully, the prisoner had picked out the third letter after every punctuation mark. He found the message:

PANEL AT EAST END OF CHAPEL SLIDES

He made quick use of the information. The panel *did* slide and Sir John slid through it to freedom.

IV   Transposition Ciphers

A transposition cipher changes the order of the letters or the words, or both. The sentence that started this book was a transposition. Each word was spelled backwards. You can write the same sentence

SAYS THIS WHAT KNOW YOU DO?
or
SYAS SIHT TAHW WONK UOY OD?

Another kind of transposition cipher is the *rail-fence* cipher. The message

YOU ARE BEING WATCHED

is written

Y U R B I G A C E
O A E E N W T H D

When professionals send enciphered messages, they generally follow certain rules that help to make the message, which they call the *clear*, more secret. To prevent the number of letters in a cipher word from giving a clue to the clear word, ciphers are written in five-letter words. To send the above rail-fence cipher, you would take off the first line and then the second line, in groups of five letters. When there are not enough letters to make the last group equal five, add on any letters at all. These extra letters are called *nulls*. The enciphered message has now become a *cryptogram*. A cryptogram is the enciphered form of any message. This one reads:

YURBI GACEO AEENW THDFL

F and L are nulls.

To decipher this cryptogram, you have to know how many nulls there are. To find out, start as if there are none. Count the letters, divide them in half, and write them down. You get

YURBIGACEO

AEENWTHDFL

If you put this into rail-fence form you get

Y U

A E

as a start. It obviously doesn't make sense, so drop one null and try again. That doesn't work either, but when you drop two nulls you easily find the clear.

Simple as this cipher seems, it was used by the Army as late as the Civil War.

A much better transposition cipher is the *route* cipher. Draw a box with any number of squares. A five-by-five square is convenient. Write the clear, in normal order, one letter to a box.

I	M	U	S	T
H	A	V	E	T
H	E	M	O	N
E	Y	B	Y	M
O	N	D	A	Y

As in the rail-fence cipher, the cryptogram is taken off in five-letter groups. Any empty spaces left in the box are filled in by nulls.

The route for taking off the cipher can be any one you decide on. Going down each column in order would give

IHHEO MAEYN UVMBD SEOYA TTNMY

Other routes might be up one column and down the

next, a zigzag path, a spiral, etc. The person who is to decipher has only to know (or discover) the route. He then makes his box, puts in the letters according to the route, and reads the clear.

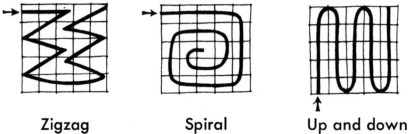

| Zigzag | Spiral | Up and down |

There are many variations of transposition ciphers and you can easily make up your own. For practice, try a column cipher. The clear is

JACK AND JILL WENT UP THE HILL

Write it in two columns.

```
J       E
A       N
C       T
K       U
A       P
N       T
D       H
J       E
I       H
L       I
L       L
W       L
```

Now take off the cipher in groups starting at the top and reading across each row. The cryptogram is

JEANC TKUAP NTDHJ EIHLI LLWLR

The final R is a null and of course it can be any letter at all.

The person who received this message would decipher it by putting the letters back into columns—if he knew the system. If he did *not* know the system, he would have to experiment until he found it. He might try rail-fence or a five-by-five square with different routes. When the results made no sense he would keep trying (hopefully!) until he found the clear in two columns.

V   The Art of the Cryptanalyst

Since an enciphered message is called a cryptogram, people who make cryptograms are called *cryptographers*. People who solve cryptograms are *cryptanalysts*.

Experienced cryptanalysts sometimes work for weeks, months, or even years to crack a cipher. Often, however, their skill is so great that within a few minutes they solve a cipher that an amateur could never solve.

How do they do it? The answer lies partly in science, partly in talent. Some of the greatest cryptanalysts in history have had a special "feeling" for ciphers that made their work seem almost magical. A brilliant guess has helped to solve many a cryptogram. But one has to start with something more dependable than a guess.

The first clue to solving a cryptogram is in the *table of frequencies*. This is simply a list of letters that tells you how often each letter is used in a certain language. If you count the number of times each letter appears on a page of a newspaper, you will find that E is the most common letter in the English language. The next most frequently used letter is T. The experts disagree about the exact order of the others, but in any case, the first nine letters in the *usual* order of frequency are E T A O N R I S H. A full table of frequencies appears at the end of this book.

In a message of more than a few sentences in length, the cryptanalyst's first step is to make a count of how many times each letter is used. Using his table of frequencies, he can guess the clear of many letters.

Here is a simple example of how it works. Suppose you are solving a cryptogram and find that the most frequently used letter is B and the next, L. You see the word LKB. Knowing that B probably stands for E, you put an E under the B

LKB
e

and a T under the L. Now you have LKB.

t – e

At this point, you stop worrying about letter frequency and take out your *table of word frequency*. (There is a short one at the end of this book.) It tells you that THE is the most common word in the English language, so you try filling in the blank in T–E with an H.

Now you test your guesses by putting T, H or E under all the L's, K's, and B's in the cryptogram. If you come across the two-letter word

K B
h e

it looks as if you are on the right track. If you find

K B N K
t h – t

you try A for N because THAT is the only word that makes sense.

Basically, this sort of trial and error is the starting point for all cipher solutions. In addition to tables of letter and word frequencies, there are tables of two- and three-letter combinations. They can be found at the end of this book, too.

With so much help, solving ciphers doesn't seem very difficult—and it wouldn't be, if ciphers weren't planned to *make* it difficult. You can see immediately that if you wrote a clear without any E's at all, the cryptanalyst would have a problem. Cryptograms that appear in magazines often use clears that have very unusual assortments of letters, such as

AJAX AND XAVIER EXITED FROM SIX ZOOS

It would not be possible to do this if you had to write a long and important message. The answer, then, is to use a cipher that *hides* the frequency of letters and words. These ciphers are *substitution ciphers* and we will see how they work in the following chapters.

VI Substitution Ciphers

About 90 percent of all ciphers are substitution ciphers. The letters of the clear are replaced by other letters, numbers, or symbols.

In a *simple substitution* the replacement for each letter is always the same. Morse code and Julius Caesar cipher are examples of this type. In Morse Code · — is always A and D is always A in Julius Caesar.

A simple substitution cipher that is well known but fun to use is the *Rosicrucian cipher.* It is based on a tic-tac-toe diagram like this:

ABC	DEF	GHI
JKL	MNO	PQR
STU	VWX	YZ

To encipher in Rosicrucian, find the letter of the clear in the diagram and draw the shape of the box it's in. Notice that no two boxes are the same. If the letter is the first one in the box, leave the box blank. If it is the second letter, put a dot in the box. If it is the third letter, put two dots in the box. To encipher

SEND HELP

you write

A variation of this cipher, known as *pigpen cipher,* uses the same diagram. The only difference is that you use dots for all the letters and put them to the left, the right, or in the center of the box to show which letter you mean. SEND HELP in pigpen is:

Pigpen breaks one of the first rules of good ciphers. Unless the dots are placed with great care the cryptogram may be very unclear. A cipher should not be confusing.

The ciphers we have done so far are simple ones. They do not hide frequencies. Now let's look at a more complicated one, a *simple substitution with suppression* *of frequencies.* This type uses more than one symbol for the very common letters, or for all of the letters. In such a cipher, G, *, or 9 might all be substitutes for E. For example, here is one in which each letter may be written three different ways.

			2	3	4	5	6	7	8	9	1
1	4	7	A	D	G	J	M	P	S	V	Y
2	5	8	B	E	H	K	N	Q	T	W	Z
3	6	9	C	F	I	L	O	R	U	X	

To encipher a letter, use any one of the numbers at the beginning of its row plus the number at the top of its column. Thus:

> A is enciphered 12, 42 or 72
> B is enciphered 22, 52 or 82
> C is enciphered 32, 62 or 92

You can easily see that such a cipher gives the cryptanalyst many more problems than a plain substitution. But this kind of cipher is only the beginning!

In the next chapter you will see an example of a *double substitution* cipher, in which the replacement of a letter is not limited to two or three symbols, but can be made by many different symbols. This type of cipher uses more than one alphabet to replace the letters of the clear.

And then there is the hardest of all to solve, the *two-step cipher*. In this type, the clear is enciphered and then it is enciphered a second time, either by substitution or some other method.

VII The Vigenère Tableau

As the use of cipher became more widespread, simple ciphers were no longer of any use when secrecy was important. There were too many people who could solve them. Governments began to employ large staffs of cryptographers to invent ciphers and cryptanalysts to crack messages from other countries and spies.

One of the great early cryptographers was Giovanni Battista della Porta, an Italian who lived from about 1538 to 1615. Della Porta invented a cipher that used twelve different alphabets. It is known as the Porta cipher.

In 1586, a Frenchman, Blaise de Vigenère, invented an even better double-substitution cipher which used twenty-six different alphabets. This cipher is still called the Vigenère cipher. It is based on a table (*tableau*, in French) known as a Vigenère tableau. Its great importance lies in the fact that it has remained the basis for many of the best ciphers throughout the years. Even

Blaise de Vigenère

though you may think that this cipher is too much trouble
to use yourself, you might like to know how it works.

A Vigenère tableau is most easily constructed on a
sheet of graph paper. First, write out the alphabet across
the top and draw a line under it. Now, start the tableau
by writing the alphabet again on the next line. Under-
neath, write another alphabet, but this time, start with
the letter B. Then start again with C. Continue in this
way until you get an alphabet that starts with Z.

Vigenère Tableau

Clear	A	B	C	D	E	F	G	H	I	J	K	L	M	N	O	P	Q	R	S	T	U	V	W	X	Y	Z
A	A	B	C	D	E	F	G	H	I	J	K	L	M	N	O	P	Q	R	S	T	U	V	W	X	Y	Z
B	B	C	D	E	F	G	H	I	J	K	L	M	N	O	P	Q	R	S	T	U	V	W	X	Y	Z	A
C	C	D	E	F	G	H	I	J	K	L	M	N	O	P	Q	R	S	T	U	V	W	X	Y	Z	A	B
D	D	E	F	G	H	I	J	K	L	M	N	O	P	Q	R	S	T	U	V	W	X	Y	Z	A	B	C
E	E	F	G	H	I	J	K	L	M	N	O	P	Q	R	S	T	U	V	W	X	Y	Z	A	B	C	D
F	F	G	H	I	J	K	L	M	N	O	P	Q	R	S	T	U	V	W	X	Y	Z	A	B	C	D	E
G	G	H	I	J	K	L	M	N	O	P	Q	R	S	T	U	V	W	X	Y	Z	A	B	C	D	E	F
H	H	I	J	K	L	M	N	O	P	Q	R	S	T	U	V	W	X	Y	Z	A	B	C	D	E	F	G
I	I	J	K	L	M	N	O	P	Q	R	S	T	U	V	W	X	Y	Z	A	B	C	D	E	F	G	H
J	J	K	L	M	N	O	P	Q	R	S	T	U	V	W	X	Y	Z	A	B	C	D	E	F	G	H	I
K	K	L	M	N	O	P	Q	R	S	T	U	V	W	X	Y	Z	A	B	C	D	E	F	G	H	I	J
L	L	M	N	O	P	Q	R	S	T	U	V	W	X	Y	Z	A	B	C	D	E	F	G	H	I	J	K

Key alphabet

L	M	N	O	P	Q	R	S	T	U	V	W	X	Y
K	L	M	N	O	P	Q	R	S	T	U	V	W	X
J	K	L	M	N	O	P	Q	R	S	T	U	V	W
I	J	K	L	M	N	O	P	Q	R	S	T	U	V
H	I	J	K	L	M	N	O	P	Q	R	S	T	U
G	H	I	J	K	L	M	N	O	P	Q	R	S	T
F	G	H	I	J	K	L	M	N	O	P	Q	R	S
E	F	G	H	I	J	K	L	M	N	O	P	Q	R
D	E	F	G	H	I	J	K	L	M	N	O	P	Q
C	D	E	F	G	H	I	J	K	L	M	N	O	P
B	C	D	E	F	G	H	I	J	K	L	M	N	O
A	B	C	D	E	F	G	H	I	J	K	L	M	N
Z	A	B	C	D	E	F	G	H	I	J	K	L	M
Y	Z	A	B	C	D	E	F	G	H	I	J	K	L
X	Y	Z	A	B	C	D	E	F	G	H	I	J	K
W	X	Y	Z	A	B	C	D	E	F	G	H	I	J
V	W	X	Y	Z	A	B	C	D	E	F	G	H	I
U	V	W	X	Y	Z	A	B	C	D	E	F	G	H
T	U	V	W	X	Y	Z	A	B	C	D	E	F	G
S	T	U	V	W	X	Y	Z	A	B	C	D	E	F
R	S	T	U	V	W	X	Y	Z	A	B	C	D	E
Q	R	S	T	U	V	W	X	Y	Z	A	B	C	D
P	Q	R	S	T	U	V	W	X	Y	Z	A	B	C
O	P	Q	R	S	T	U	V	W	X	Y	Z	A	B
N	O	P	Q	R	S	T	U	V	W	X	Y	Z	A
M	N	O	P	Q	R	S	T	U	V	W	X	Y	Z

M	N	O	P	Q	R	S	T	U	V	W	X	Y	Z

When all of the alphabets are written, make a key alphabet down the left-hand side of the tableau. The key is simply the first letter of each alphabet.

Now the tableau is finished and you are ready to encipher your message. First you will need a *key word*. Pick any word that has no repeated letters. It may be of any length and the number of alphabets used will be the same as the number of letters in the key word.

For our example, let's use STORE as the key word. The cipher will then use five alphabets.

First, write out the clear of the message.

I AM IN TROUBLE PLEASE SEND HELP AT ONCE

Now, write the key word above the message, letter for letter. Repeat the key word as many times as necessary.

storestorestorestorestorest
IAMINTROUBLEPLEASESENDHELPATONCE

The first letter of the clear is I. The key word letter above it is S. That means that you must use the S alphabet. Find S on the key alphabet and put a ruler or a sheet of paper under the S alphabet so you don't get mixed up. Now look along the alphabet at the top to find the letter I. (This is called the "clear alphabet" because you use it for the letters of the clear.) Move down the I column to the S alphabet. The cipher letter is A.

The second letter of the clear is A and the key letter above it is T. Find the T alphabet, put your ruler under it, and then locate A on the clear alphabet. Run down the column to the ruler and the cipher letter is T. In the same way, encipher M on the O alphabet, I on the R alphabet, and so on.

The final cryptogram is:

ATAZR LKCLF DXDCI SLSJI FWVVP HTHFR UXDYC

The last three letters are nulls.

Vigenère called his cipher an "indecipherable cipher" —and for many, many years, it remained exactly that.

VIII   The Rise of the Art

During the early years of the seventeenth century, France was torn with strife. There were conflicts between the Protestants and the Catholics, between the nobles and the monarchy. There was spying, intrigue and betrayal on all sides.

It was at this time of unrest, in the year 1628, that the town of Réalmont was under seige by the Prince of Condé. A man was captured while trying to sneak through the battle lines. No one was safe from suspicion and the man was searched. He had in his pocket a poem— a poem so badly written that even the soldiers who made the search didn't believe that anyone would write such miserable poetry. They turned it over to the cipher experts in Condé's army. The experts agreed that it was the worst poem that they had ever seen—but they also agreed that if it was a cipher, they couldn't solve it.

Then, someone remembered that there lived nearby a gentleman named Antoine Rossignol. His hobby was cryptography.

Rossignol was called in and within a few hours he had found the cipher message in the poem. It came from the commander of Réalmont and said that the town could not hold out much longer because it was running out of ammunition. When Condé sent the cipher together with the clear to Réalmont, the town surrendered at once. The surrender was of historical importance, but not nearly as much importance as the discovery of Rossignol. He proved to be one of the greatest cryptanalysts the world has ever known.

Antoine Rossignol

Rossignol never told anyone how he deciphered. But it was plain that he had a brilliant mind together with a genuine gift for cryptanalysis. No secret message was safe if it fell into Rossignol's hands.

Under the reign of Louis XIV of France, Rossignol established one of the greatest cryptographic offices in the world. Not content with deciphering, Rossignol worked out a new cipher for use by the French diplomatic service. It was known as the Great Cipher of Louis XIV and more than two hundred years were to pass before anyone solved it. The man who finally did was another Frenchman, and like Rossignol, one of the greatest cryptanalysts of all time. His name was Étienne Bazeries.

Rossignol lived to be 83 years old. Under his leadership, the art of cipher flourished and many brilliant cryptographers came to light in France and in other countries.

There were also some who were not so brilliant, however. Outstanding among them was the Chevalier De Rohan. He was a French army officer who constantly boasted about his skill at deciphering.

While De Rohan was in charge of guarding a border town against the Dutch, the enemy offered him a large sum of money if he would allow the town to be captured. De Rohan needed money badly and he decided to betray his country. He told his plans to his aide and sent him to make the final arrangements with the Dutch.

But the French were suspicious, and one dark night they seized both De Rohan and the aide and placed them under arrest. De Rohan swore that he was innocent and he knew that his officers had no proof against him unless the aide confessed. The big question was, would the aide betray him? There didn't seem to be any way to find out.

One day, as he sat in his prison cell in the Bastille, De Rohan received a package of shirts from a friend. There was a message written on one shirt sleeve. It said:

MG DULHXCCLGU GHJ YXUJ LM CT ULGC ALJ

De Rohan stared at the message for days and could make nothing of it. In spite of his many boasts about his skill as a cryptanalyst, he could not figure out the simple substitution cipher, which is very easily solved with a table of French letter frequencies. The message said:

LE PRISONNIER EST MORT IL N'A RIEN DIT

which in English means

THE PRISONER IS DEAD HE HAS SAID NOTHING

When he went before the court, unaware that his secret was safe, De Rohan confessed all. He lost his head because he couldn't solve a cipher!

IX Playfair

After the time of Louis XIV and until the start of the twentieth century, the art of the cipher had its ups and downs. Interest came and went, and so did fads in ciphers. But at the start of World War I, every country became aware of the need for safe ciphers and good cryptanalysts. Most of the ciphers in use at that time were elaborate variations of the Vigenère. Then, suddenly, England came up with something really new. It was called the Playfair cipher. Actually, there were reports that England had had this cipher for a good many years, but had kept it secret.

Playfair is based on a key word written into a five-by-five square. This is followed by all of the letters of the alphabet in order, skipping letters that have already appeared in the key word. Let's use APRICOT as the key word and fill out the square.

A	P	R	I	C
O	T	B	D	E
F	G	H	J-K	L
M	N	Q	S	U
V	W	X	Y	Z

It is usual to put I and J in the same box, because there are only twenty-five boxes in the square, but since I appears in the key word, J and K share a box instead.

Now the clear is written out and divided into two-letter groups.

LEAVE TONIGHT
LE AV ET ON IG HT

If double letters fall together in the same pair, put in a null X to separate them. STEEP becomes ST, EX, EP.

Now you are ready to begin. Look at the first pair of letters in the clear, LE. Notice that they both fall in the same column (up and down) of the square. To encipher them, you write down the letter that comes below each of them in the column. Since U falls below L, and L falls below E, LE becomes UL.

If a letter falls at the bottom of a column, use the letter at the top of that column. Thus, AV, the next two letters of the clear, becomes OA.

When the letters are in the same row (across) of the square, you take the letter to the right of each one. If a letter falls at the end of a row, you take the *first* letter in that same row. The next pair in the clear, ET, becomes OB.

If the letters are neither in the same row nor the same column, it becomes more complicated. You draw an imaginary rectangle around the letters in the square, and use the letters in the opposite corners of the rectangle for the cipher. *Use the letter in the same row first.* To encipher ON, you would draw a rectangle and find that the letters in the opposite corners are M and T. The cipher reads TM (*not* MT). In the same way, IG becomes PK, and HT is GB.

The completed cryptogram, in five-letter units, is:

ULOAO BTMPK GBLFR

The last three letters are nulls.

Playfair was used very successfully for a little while and was extremely popular because it is so easy to use. However, it turned out to be unsafe. One of its flaws is that the cipher for any pair in the clear is always the same for that pair. In a long message, this gives valuable clues. It turns out that with a table of *digram* (two-letter combinations) frequencies, Playfair is not difficult for a good cryptanalyst to solve.

X Ciphers in Our Century

As early as the time of the American Civil War it was clear that simple word-of-mouth orders were no longer very useful in military matters. Armies were large and scattered. The telegraph had been invented and fast communications were possible and needed. But they had to be secret.

Never before had there been such interest in secret writing as there was by the turn of the century. There were many new ciphers and all sorts of machines to make their use easier and more accurate.

Sir Francis Beaufort in England simplified the Vigenère tableau. The St. Cyr ruler, invented in France, was a slide rule that worked out Vigenère mechanically with less chance of error. Unfortunately for both of these developments, a German named Kasiski had devised a method for solving Vigenère ciphers in 1863. Since he published a book on his method, it was hardly a secret any more.

Disc cipher machines with alphabets printed on the edges of turning discs became popular, too.

Ciphers and gadgets appeared and disappeared until the outbreak of World War I. Spies were everywhere; secret messages were passed at the rate of hundreds a day. So pressing was the need for safe ciphers and for excellent cryptanalysis that the war has sometimes been called the War of the Cryptographers.

The center of United States cryptography following World War I was known as the American Black Chamber. It was founded by a very unusual man.

Herbert Osborne Yardley was born in Indiana in 1889. When he was 23 years old he became a code clerk in the State Department. One day a message came through for President Wilson and Yardley tried to solve the code just to see if he could. Within a few hours he had done it.

His fame spread and as soon as America declared war in 1917, Yardley was made head of the Cryptography Department of Military Intelligence. When the war ended in 1918, Yardley went to Europe to see what he could learn there. On his return in 1919, the American Black Chamber was born.

In its first year, the Black Chamber deciphered 813 Japanese telegrams, which were enciphered in eleven different systems. Between then and 1929, when it was dissolved, the Chamber deciphered over 45,000 telegrams from many different countries in as many different languages.

After his retirement, Yardley wrote a number of books about his work and they have become classics for those interested in cryptography.

More recently, the United States has been proud of another great cryptanalyst. Many people think he is the greatest cryptanalyst of all time. His name is William Frederick Friedman. Much of his finest work was done together with his wife Elizebeth. Friedman was the Chief Cryptographer for the United States during World War II. One of his brilliant feats during the early part of the war was to break the Japanese code known as *Purple*.

Purple was a machine code. The machine consisted of two typewriters connected by a complicated system of wiring. As the clear was typed on one typewriter, an electrically controlled turning drum kept changing the alphabet that was used to print out the cryptogram on the other typewriter.

Purple was an extremely difficult cipher to break. Friedman and his men put in months of ceaseless work before they thought they had the problem solved. Then they built a machine to unscramble the Japanese messages. Although these men had never seen the Japanese

Purple machine, the one they built was almost exactly like it—and of course it did the job perfectly.

Almost all important ciphers today use electronic machines of one sort or another. Literally the entire world (and part of space, too) is crisscrossed with radio circuits, telephone, telegraph, television and radar networks. In the United States, the National Security Agency is in charge of monitoring all of these systems. N.S.A. is a fantastically large and busy cryptologic agency.

It is possible that N.S.A. uses more computers than any other organization in the world. A computer, of course, can do in seconds what it might take a man years to do. It can store all of the frequency tables in every language and it can try out and discard thousands upon thousands of letter combinations a minute.

Even so, computers are only aids. They cannot do the whole job. This is true both in creating ciphers and in deciphering. The special talent, the brilliant guess of the unusual cryptanalyst, is something the computer cannot match. The professional cryptanalyst today saves time with a computer. But in the end, like a cryptanalyst of several hundred years ago—and like you—he says, "Could Y stand for F? Or might it be . . . ?"

Appendix

LETTER		Approximate number of times this letter occurs in 100 letters. Since no fractions are used, several groups of frequency numbers appear to be identical. They are not. Each letter occurs less often than the letter above it.
1.	E	13
2.	T	10
3.	A	8
4.	O	8
5.	N	7
6.	R	7
7.	I	6

8.	S	6
9.	H	5
10.	D	4
11.	L	3
12.	F	3
13.	C	3
14.	M	3
15.	U	2
16.	G	2
17.	Y	2
18.	P	2
19.	W	
20.	B	
21.	V	
22.	K	
23.	X	All less than two, in this order.
24.	J	
25.	Q	
26.	Z	

TABLE OF WORD FREQUENCIES

Some common English words in order of use.

THE	OR
OF	HER
AND	HAD
TO	AT
A	FROM
IN	THIS
THAT	MY
IS	THEY
I	ALL
IT	THEIR
FOR	AN
AS	SHE
WITH	HAS
WAS	WERE
HIS	ME
HE	BEEN
BE	HIM
NOT	ONE
BY	SO
BUT	IF
HAVE	WILL
YOU	THERE
WHICH	WHO
ARE	NO
ON	

Two-letter combinations in order of use.

TH	RA
IN	RO
ER	LI
RE	RI
AN	IO
HE	LE
AR	ND
EN	MA
TI	SE
TE	AL
AT	IC
ON	FO
HA	IL
OU	NE
IT	LA
ES	TA
ST	EL
OR	ME
NT	EC
HI	IS
EA	DI
VE	SI
CO	CA
DE	

TABLE OF ENGLISH TRIGRAM FREQUENCIES

Three-letter combinations in order of use.

THE	CON
ING	NCE
AND	ALL
ION	EVE
ENT	ITH
FOR	TED
TIO	AIN
ERE	EST
HER	MAN
ATE	RED
VER	THI
TER	IVE
THA	REA
ATI	WIT
HAT	ONS
ERS	ESS
HIS	AVE
RES	PER
ILL	ECT
ARE	ONE

Index

frequencies, English digram, 58
frequencies, English trigram, 59
frequencies, letter, 27
frequencies, suppression of, 31–32
frequencies, word, 28
Friedman, E., 51
Friedman, W.F., 51

grill cipher, 15–17

International Morse Code, 2
invisible ink, 14

Julius Caesar cipher, 5, 30

Kasiski, 49

machine code, 51–52
machine, disc cipher, 50
Morse code, 1–2, 30

National Security Agency, 52–53
N.S.A., 52–53

peccavi, 11
pigpen cipher, 31
Playfair cipher, 46–48
Porta cipher, 34
Purple, 51–52

rail-fence cipher, 22–23
Rosicrucian cipher, 30–31
Rossignol, 41–43
route cipher, 23–24

St. Cyr ruler, 49
shopkeeper's cipher, 6–8
shopkeeper's code, 6–8
simple substitution cipher, 30
substitution ciphers, 29, 30–48
substitution, double, 32
suppression of frequencies, 31–32